The Ultimate Guide to Buying a Home in Flower Mound

THE "BIG" SMALL TOWN WITH AN
AMAZING QUALITY OF LIFE

Nicole Smith Woodard

fantasticdfwhomes.com

Nicole Smith Woodard
nicole@nicolesmith.net

Ordering Information:
Quantity sales. Special discounts are available on quantity purchases by corporations, associations, and others. For details, contact the "Special Sales Department" at the address above.

The Ultimate Guide to Buying a home in Flower Mound/ Nicole Smith Woodard. —1st ed.
ISBN 978-0-9904941-7-1

Contents

Flower Mound is, hands-down, one of the most special communities in the Dallas/Fort Worth Metroplex, offering residents a stellar overall quality of life thanks to:

- Top-rated schools
- Plentiful parks and outdoor recreation areas (54 in all!)
- Community activities
- Dog parks
- Grapevine Lake – its view, marinas and trails
- Preserved natural areas and open space
- Sports facilities, including a golf course
- Easy commutes to both downtown Fort Worth, Dallas, and all other major employment centers
- Just 4 miles to DFW International Airport
- Convenient shopping
- Top-notch dining
- Lowest area property taxes
- Family friendly events and activities
- Well-maintained public spaces

- Beautiful homes and landscaped medians and neighborhoods at all price points
- And so much more...

All these features in an area that is an oasis of peace and tranquility that was first settled in the 1840s. In fact, most of the town, which is located along the northern shore of scenic Grapevine Lake, is connected by walking and biking trails.

You feel like you're in the country, yet are very close the "big city" and all that it offers (although you can get everything you need close to home). Dallas is just 20 miles to the southeast; Fort Worth is 25 miles to the southwest. The town is mostly within Denton County, with a small portion in Tarrant County.

Within the town boundaries, there are lots of distinct neighborhoods that have been developed over the years, each offering its own unique benefits and amenities.

There are areas in Flower Mound where you can buy a 1,500-square-foot home built in the 1980s, as well as areas offering homes upwards of five acres or located within an exclusive gated community.

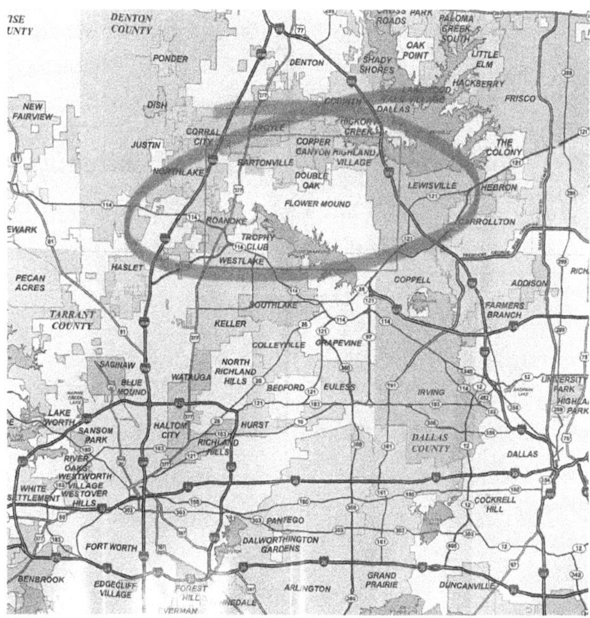

There are always options available for purchase in all areas of the housing spectrum: pre-owned homes, new homes, communities where you can build... single family homes, luxury estates, condos, townhomes— it's all here. Families, young professionals, over 55... everyone is welcome here.

With single-family homes ranging in price from the mid-$200,000s to well over $1 million, and a variety of architectural styles and sizes, anybody can find their dream home in the town of Flower Mound. The average sale price in Flower Mound in 2020 is around $450,000, compared to the average price in the DFW Metroplex of approximately $335,000.

The population of Flower Mound is currently around 75,000 within its 43.4 square miles, with more new residents moving in regularly as they fall in love with its charm.

The local government's smart growth system for urban planning ensures that what has made Flower Mound special won't be endangered even as it grows in population. That is just one of the reasons Flower Mound is known as a "big" small town.

The quality of life and other advantages of Flower Mound have been recognized nationwide.

Flower Mound has been named:

- #4 Safest City in Texas by LendEDU in 2020
- #1 Safest City in Texas by SafeHome in 2019
- #1 Safest City with a Population Over 50,000 by Home Security Advisor in 2019
- #2 Happiest Small Town in America by Top Counseling Schools in 2019
- #1 Most Livable Small City in the U.S. by SmartAsset in 2019
- #1 Best City to Live in Texas by Chamber-ofCommerce.org in 2019

And that's just a small taste of the many accolades it has received over the years, including a Platinum Level Scenic City Certification earned in 2019 which recognized the town's efforts to set high-quality standard for the appearance of public spaces and its impact on property values and economic development.

Needless to say, Flower Mound is getting a lot of attention! Now, let's get into the details.

There is a wide variety of home styles and price points, amenities, convenience, and more.

Let's take a tour of all that Flower Mound has to offer.

What's in the Name?

Flower Mound is named after a 50-foot tall mound covering 12.5 acres located in the center of town. A natural formation, it is typically covered in grass and dozens of varieties of bright wildflowers.

Bridlewood – The Centerpiece Community

Developed in the 1990s, Bridlewood has been the flagship neighborhood of Flower Mound that set the standard of excellence for future development. It's located in the center of town, making everything within easy reach here, including on-site elementary and middle schools.

Bridlewood is built around its golf course. But, that's far from the only recreational facilities here. There are also tennis courts, basketball courts, a fitness center, and two outdoor pools– perfect to cool off in that Texas summer heat.

There are 11 different communities within Bridlewood, offering a range of home architectural styles and sizes that give each phase a signature look. Home construction started in the 1990s and finished in the early 2000s, which also influences the look of the homes here. Many homes in Bridlewood have their own pool.

Home prices in Bridlewood range from the low $400,000s to well over $1.2 million.

Outdoor areas range from small yards to lots over an acre (with estate-style homes to match) in the Bridlewood Farms community, which also contains the Bridlewood Stables and Equestrian Center.

This showcase facility has 45 stalls, boarding facilities, and covered riding area, as well as lessons for students of all ages. Perfect for all the horse enthusiasts who want to be close to their horses while enjoying the modern conveniences of a community.

The Belmont phase, for example, is closest to the middle school. It is also adjacent to the "back entrance" in the northernmost point of Bridlewood which puts it within a quick drive of The Shops at Highland Village, a plaza that features Super Target and other shops and restaurants.

Wellington – Master Planned & Active

One of the largest developments within Flower Mound, Wellington, has 2,400 + homes constructed between 1995 and 2015.

There is a wide variety of homes available here, including smaller homes ideal for first-time homebuyers, those seeking to downsize, or those on a budget who want that desirable Flower Mound address. There are plenty of larger and more luxury homes in Wellington as well.

Its location on the south side of Flower Mound gives Wellington homeowners quick access to DFW airport and major freeways.

For those with an active lifestyle, this community could be perfect with its nine-hole disc golf course and two fitness centers offering Olympic-sized swimming pools.

Home prices in Wellington range from the low $400,000s to mid $600,000s. Most homes are brick and feature some siding, stone or rock, which is a very popular style in Texas. Most homeowners here have invested the effort and expense to maintain and improve their homes.

One thing to note is that there is a lot of "movement" in the Wellington real estate market, with more than 100 homes selling every six months. That means plenty of opportunity for buyers to find their perfect home in this neighborhood.

CHAPTER 3

Riverwalk at Flower Mound – The New Kid on the Block

In the heart of Flower Mound, you find the unique –
and still under development – mixed-use community of

Riverwalk. Unlike the original subdivisions in town, there is a variety of housing options, from single family homes with backyards, to townhomes, to apartments for lease.

Riverwalk is a walkable, accessible community. The centerpiece is the man-made river that runs through it, lined with walking paths, restaurants (coming soon!), and residential units. It's a connection point and gathering place for the community. With its small-town feel and public spaces, you can expect plenty of community events and celebrations. And you'll definitely want to check out the expressive public art.

By leasing an apartment, you can take your time in investigating this neighborhood and all the others in Flower Mound to see which you ultimately want to settle in– not to mention, you'll have your finger on the pulse of the area's real estate market. It's the perfect way to "get your feet wet" in Flower Mound.

Lakeside DFW – A Mixed-Use, Walkable Community

Lakeside DFW is a mixed-use community at the southern end of Flower Mound. It is truly one-of-a-kind and attracts people from all over the metroplex. There are single-family homes and multi-family apartments, townhomes for purchase and/or lease, and a truly spectacular luxury condo tower with views of the lake. You'll also find boutiques and restaurants in Lakeside, as well as a dine-in movie theater and Starbucks.

Views of Grapevine Lake and its walking and biking trails on its shores is a plus. Community activities are another benefit, with live music every Friday, weather permitting.

It's easy to live, work, and play here. With its walkability, Lakeside is a very welcoming area where you can get to know your neighbors.

The villa homes have a zero lot line on one side and five-foot side yards on the other, with rear-entry garages. Most of the traditional homes are set on quarter-acre plus lots. Prices range from the low $500,000s to well over $1,000,000.

The final phase of Lakeside, Lakeside Village, has received zoning approval, and the infrastructure is under construction. This development is definitely worth watching. These luxury villa-style homes will start around $1.2 million. Currently, there are luxury townhomes available here, starting at around $600,000.

This continues to be a rapidly selling community, much like it began. In 2014, there were only 240 single family lots available, and there were three different builders with a waiting list of 50 to 60 people at any given time. As the builders released blocks of lots, they were snatched up quickly and homes were built.

A big advantage to Lakeside is that it lies at the southern end of Flower Mound, so it's a quick 15-minute drive on the highway to DFW International Airport, as well as its easy access to all points in the Metroplex via the expansive highway system.

They say that you tell how well a home will resale by looking at how properties in the neighborhood sold to begin with. So that bodes well for Lakeside, Wellington, Bridlewood, and most Flower Mound communities.

Luxury Homes Near Grapevine Lake

As you've seen, there is a wide variety of housing styles and price points available in Flower Mound. That extends to an area of luxury homes adjacent to Grapevine

Lake that features a truly beautiful landscape– a blend of mature trees and sprawling hills.

There are high-end gated communities here, including Chateau du Lac, Point Noble, and The Landing, where 1-acre plus lot sizes offer additional privacy.

The homes, of course, are also spacious, with some built 20 years ago and other brand new masterpieces of contemporary design. Those looking for luxury, privacy, and proximity DFW and well-regarded public and private schools, will find a home in these developments.

CHAPTER 6

How to Buy a Home

Since you've found your way to this guide to *Buying a Home in Flower Mound*, I'm making the assumption you've already decided to buy a home. Good for you! To affirm that decision, consider these two key facts:

1. **Buying a Home Is a Great investment** – Real estate, unlike stocks and bonds, is a tangible asset. It is typical that the equity in your home will ultimately represent a major percentage of your net worth.

2. **Buying a Home Is Good for You and Your Family** – Quite simply, owning a home represents *freedom*. Freedom from rent increases and someone else making decisions about your housing costs. Freedom to decorate and improve to your heart's content without a

landlord telling you what you can and cannot do. And, most importantly, when you own a home, you have a permanent place to build memories.

Our homes create chapters in the story of our lives, and owning a home allows you to bring stability to this chapter.

There are countless how-to-buy-a-home resources available to you. It's overwhelming. But, in this guide, I'm going to focus on the key things you need to know and do when buying a home.

Follow these strategies and your homebuying process will be much smoother from the beginning of your search all the way to the day you get the keys to your new home.

Find and Work with Professionals You Can Trust

You may be thinking that you don't need a real estate agent, right? The data is available on countless websites. When you see a sign in the yard, you can pull up the details on the app in your phone. Some sites even offer immediate showings.

Here's the deal: Finding the home is the easiest part. Getting it under contract– believe it or not, even in this environment of multiple offers– is the second easiest part. Keeping the contract together all the way to a successful closing is the hard part, and that's where having the right real estate agent represent you is essential.

I promise you that the quality of your homebuying experience will be directly related to the quality of professionals involved.

Things change rapidly in the real estate market. Whether you are buying your first home or your first home in a while, this is a very complex process. You need someone working for you who is full-time, knee-deep immersed in the everyday business of helping people buy houses.

You need someone who will be an excellent negotiator on your behalf and will educate you every step of the way.

Where can you find the right agent?

1. Get referrals and recommendations from friends, family, co-workers, and neighbors.
2. Research potential candidates by checking out their website, review sites, and other online profiles, including social media.
3. Make contact with potential agents and request references.
4. Interview a few different agents to find the right one for you, asking questions inspired by the list below.

What qualities are you looking for in your real estate agent?

1. At a minimum, the agent you choose should be licensed and certified. Additional education and training is a good sign, too.
2. Your agent should have a strong track record and a "healthy" amount of listings (not so many that they don't have time for you).

3. Experience counts for a lot but so does personality and chemistry. Find somebody you "gel" with and can see yourself working with for the next few months.

4. Make sure the agent has experience in the neighborhoods you are interested in. He or she needs to know trends, specific listings that might fit you, and more.

5. Your agent must be transparent. They should be working on your behalf, not for their own benefit.

6. Honesty is vital. They should be open with you – not afraid to tell you the truth instead of what you want to hear.

7. Responsiveness and customer service is key. When you have questions or concerns, your agent should get back to you ASAP.

8. Your agent should be proactive – bringing you listings that fit your criteria, not waiting for you to request them.

9. The agent should be able to give you insight on market performance in different neighborhoods to help you protect your investment.

Finding the right agent can make the homebuying process easier and less stressful. It is definitely worth making the effort at the outset to find the perfect person for the job.

Beyond Your Real Estate Agent

There are so many things that can go awry during the homebuying process from beginning to end... and even after. When it comes to things going wrong, it's not "if..." it's "when." The difference between you getting the home you want easily - or getting so discouraged you stop the process and give up... or continuing through an absolutely horrific process- is directly related to the professionals you choose to work with.

I'm not just talking about the real estate agent you choose, but also the lender, home inspector, appraiser, title attorney, repair professionals, mover, utility concierge, cleaning company, home warranty company – and it all starts with your real estate agent.

A great real estate agent knows who's who and what's what and connects you with professionals most likely to make your process seamless and pleasurable during this very stressful experience. A quality agent is there for you every step of the way during the homebuying process and even after the papers are signed (more details on that later in this chapter).

Once you become a homeowner, a relationship with a great real estate agent is vital. There's a lot to being a homeowner!

Once you've identified the real estate professional you want to work for you, it's time to find your lender. Start with the lender recommended by your real estate agent.

There are many reasons to use a local lender versus an online lending portal, but that's for a different book. The first thing you should do is get pre-approved for your mortgage. Absolutely no looking at houses before getting pre-approved!!

Once you know the mortgage amount you qualify for and the price you can comfortably afford to pay for your new home, you'll want to crystalize your must-have list.

Putting Together Your Wish List

You've probably dreamed about what your new home will look like and how you'll feel living in it. You now get to decide what you need:

- Number of bedrooms
- Number of bathrooms
- Garage size

Do you want:

- An open floorplan or more segmented space?
- A big yard with room to roam or a small low-maintenance yard?
- A swimming pool or not?
- A front or side facing garage?
- One or two stories?

Focus on things you can't easily change, such as location and floorplan.

Cosmetic things like flooring, paint, counters, etc., can easily be altered – and likely will be – during the course of your ownership as styles and trends change and as the needs of you and your family change.

Where Do You Want to Live?

As you go through the homebuying process, you must determine the community or communities you will focus on.

Truth be told, the house can be absolutely perfect, but if it's not in the right community for you, it doesn't matter. I've driven folks all over the Dallas/Fort Worth

Metroplex chasing the perfect "house," only for them to be sorely disappointed when they realize the area the house is in is less than desirable, for whatever reason.

Consider your needs:

- How far are you willing to commute to your job each day?
- Are there certain activities – such as golf, tennis, church, hiking – that you'll want to live super close to?
- How important is speedy access to healthcare providers?
- Do you want fine dining options and high-end shopping available close to you?
- Do you have children in school? If so, what are the most important criteria for you when considering the schools your children will attend? Academics? Fine Arts? Athletics?
- What do you like to do in your spare time?
- Are you looking for a tight-knit community with lots of kids and activities, or are you more interested in a wider, open, rural feel with space between you and your nearest neighbor?

Only you can answer these questions for you, and the answers may change between the time you start your search and actually buy your home.

Searching for Your Dream Home

Once you know your price, your area, and your criteria, it's time to hit the streets – after searching for homes on the apps and websites online. Your agent can help expedite this process, too, by setting you up to receive alerts directly from the multiple listing service (MLS) so you don't have to scroll through all of the homes you've already eliminated from consideration.

What you'll find very quickly is that the websites are great resources, but there is no substitute for actually driving by the home – you're seeking more than just a home, you're buying in to a community.

As you drive around, you will find neighborhoods and communities that resonate with you and others that don't. And that's okay.

The house you buy is so much more than sticks and bricks– it's your home, your identity, where you'll spend the next few years (or decades) of your life. You'll want to feel good when you drive down that street, see your home from a distance, pull in the driveway, and be "home."

This must be done in person. Side note: Don't ever call the agent whose name is on the sign in front of the home. They have been hired by the seller to get it sold for top dollar. This is where you get the agent you've selected to represent you involved.

When you find the home for you, you'll know it. And, if you're working with a great professional, they'll help you get it.

I tell my clients that I have no preference on WHICH house they pick– it's theirs. You'll be paying for it. You'll be living in it. I make no judgments on which house you pick. But once you pick a house, I'm going to help you get it.

Side note: I will not render my opinion on whether or not you'll be happy in your new home or whether or not this floorplan will work for you. But I will provide feedback on future resale implications. If it's backing to a busy street or there are planes flying overhead (welcome to Flower Mound!), those dynamics may not be an issue for you. But, they could be issues for future resale, and I'll point that out as you view each home.

So when you call me several years later– ready to buy your next home with my help – you'll know in advance, from the discussions we'll have as you're purchasing, any potential resale issues that may need to be considered when selling.

What to Do After You've Found the Right Home

Once you've found the perfect home for you (there are no "perfect homes," but I contend there is a "perfect home for you"), it's time to go get it.

As I tell my clients, there is no pressure– ever– to buy a particular home. There is, however, urgency. Once you've decided you want a home to be yours, do not delay in pursuing it. The house you see today and consider tonight may very well be the one someone else saw yesterday and will pursue today.

Your agent can advise you how to structure an offer that is likely to be accepted by the seller. Once the offer is accepted, there will be inspections. All houses have issues and all issues can be fixed - it's just a matter of who's going to pay for it. And everything is negotiable.

Simultaneously, you'll be asked to provide all kinds of documentation to your mortgage lender, shop for homeowner's insurance, and prepare for the move.

The closing process is relatively easy, and then the fun begins. That's my favorite part of the entire process – it's why I work in real estate.

It's like the last 30 seconds of the "House Hunters" episode when the family and their friends are gathered around the kitchen island or on the back patio enjoying the lovely new home – and life – they now live.

In the case of my clients, that's also when my real work begins.

I believe in supporting my clients in their decision to become homeowners and continuing to bring value to them throughout their ownership. Here's how:

- Each year I send a full account of all homes that sold in their neighborhood to help them keep an eye on the value of their home.
- Each month my clients receive a newsletter with market data, keeping them knowledgeable about what's going on in the real estate market in our area.
- I provide information when the tax assessments are mailed each spring so they can proactively protest the value and save some money each year on property taxes.

- I love to connect my clients with professionals for anything home-related, such as decorators, painters, flooring companies, handymen, electricians, landscapers, and others.
- I am also a connector within the local community. I know the best financial advisors, CPAs, dentists, doctors, attorneys, and more, and love to connect my clients with the best in the area.
- And, at least once a year, I find a way to meet with them in person to share life. It's what I do, and it's what I love.

Now… to you. Thank you for taking the time to digest this information.

Congratulations on making the decision to buy a home– whether in Flower Mound or wherever your ideal community is.

Please consider me your real estate resource. If there is ever anything I can do for you, please contact me. It would be my pleasure to include you as one of my happy clients.

You can reach me at www.FantasticDFWHomes.com or by calling 682-472-2473.

CHAPTER 7

The Questions You Should Ask Real Estate Agents Before Hiring Them

There is no shortage of real estate professionals in the Dallas Metroplex. How do you pick the right one for you? How do you make sure they have the skills and experience to help you find and buy your dream home?

Experience and area knowledge are just the start of the qualifications you should be looking for.

Use the questions below to interview potential real estate agents to help you find – and successfully buy – the right home at the right price for your family in a timely manner. I've included my responses to share my experience and what sets me apart from other real estate agents you may consider hiring to represent you in Flower Mound or the surrounding areas.

How long have you been a full-time real estate agent?

I have been helping families buy and sell houses in the Dallas/Fort Worth Metroplex since 1995. I went to college in Fort Worth, and, except for a couple of year hiatus in south Texas in the early 1990s, I have been a lifelong resident of the Metroplex. I spent about 20 years in Southlake, and then I built a house in Flower Mound in 2014.

How many homes do you close each year?

As a solo agent with a full-time assistant, I close anywhere between 30 to 40 houses each and every year.

As the homebuyer, who will be my primary point of contact?

I will always be your primary point of contact. All communication goes directly through me. I have an assistant who helps me behind the scenes to make sure all the t's are crossed and the i's are dotted. You'll always deal directly with me.

What qualities or certifications set you apart from other agents?

Having helped 30 to 40 families a year now for the past 25 years, it's highly unusual that a situation comes up that I haven't already seen based on my experience or that I can't immediately find a resource to take care of. So, longevity is one differentiator, certainly when compared to an agent just getting started in this very complex business.

Even with my years of experience, I believe that a real estate professional should constantly be learning and building knowledge of the industry. I take education very, very seriously. I am a licensed real estate Broker, which yields an elevated level of knowledge, responsibility and accountability vs someone who is a licensed real estate Agent. I have earned numerous industry designations including becoming a Certified Luxury Home Marketing Specialist, and I'm in the Million Dollar GUILD. This certification, and the information and the knowledge that comes with the certification and experience, allows me to market very high-end luxury homes. It is my belief that once an agent has the knowledge and experience to serve luxury homeowners, it is imperative that I bring a luxury level of marketing to homes of any price point.

I am a Certified Real Estate Divorce specialist, which means I have education, training and experience helping couples who find themselves going through the divorce process while buying or selling a home. It's certainly not fun or what anybody wants to do. Buying or selling a home is already pretty stressful and when you compound that with the dissolving of a marriage, there are numerous other challenges that come with it that I'm specifically trained to manage.

DMagazine, Fort Worth Magazine, Texas Monthly Magazine, and Fort Worth Business Press have all recognized me as a top producing real estate agent in the area consistently for the past 15+ years.

I'm also a Certified Relocation Specialist and, as such, have had a lot of experience with clients who are relocating to and from the Dallas/Fort Worth area.

How can you help me buy a home in a competitive market?

We have had a competitive market here in the Dallas/Fort Worth area, no doubt, since coming out of the recession around 2012.

But you could argue that for all of the 25+ years I've been helping families, it has always a "competitive" market, because I want my clients to win.

If you're a seller, I want you to get top dollar as quickly as possible for your property. We want to compete against your neighbors and win.

If you're a buyer, certainly for the last seven, eight years where the supply and demand scenario has been so tilted in favor of the sellers, I want to get the house you want for the best price possible (and sometimes the "best price" is list price or greater).

One of the things that you'll find when you work with me – whether you are buying or selling (or both at the same time) -- is I will educate you every step of the way on what you can expect. You'll be very well-educated about the dynamics in the market and how we will position you to win.

For example, if you're a buyer client of mine, every time I show you a house, I will bring a quick market analysis of the community so you can know right then and there if the home we're viewing is one of the highest-priced homes in the community or, conversely, if it is priced very competitively and likely to sell at multiple offers. When you find the house you're looking for, I can help you structure an offer that will compete and, most likely, win.

On the other end, if you're selling your home, my pricing presentation is usually about a quarter inch thick stack of paper. We go through it together, and I educate you on the way I recommend we position your home in the market to sell for top dollar.

These are the processes and systems that I have been consistently improving over the past 25+ years. You'll get the benefit of me having already worked out quite a lot of the kinks along the way. What I bring to you is tried and true. It's proven; it's effective. And I can almost always guarantee you the results.

How do you communicate with your clients?

One of the first questions I'll ask you is how you want to be communicated with. Certainly some of my clients want voice-to-voice contact over the phone. Others want to be texted, and some want to be emailed. However you want to be communicated with is how I will communicate with you.

How do you set realistic expectations for your clients?

One of the first things we do when we meet is to discuss your goals. From there, I will educate you about the dynamics in this market, and what it will likely take to meet your goals. I will bring all of my years of experience and the systems that I've worked through successfully for others to you - for your benefit.

What neighborhoods do you specialize in?

I specialize in the Flower Mound community, whether that is a zero-lot-line home in Lakeside, a luxury property on acreage on the lake, or a home in a master-planned neighborhood like Wellington or Bridlewood -- and all of the other desirable communities Flower Mound offers. Of course, being where we are in proximity to DFW airport and all the major employment centers, I have experience in many of the surrounding communities as well. But first and foremost, Flower Mound is my place.

What's your schedule and availability?

My commitment is to respond to you in a timely manner. If there is a house that you want to view, I will commit to getting you access to it within the next 24 hours. If I'm not personally available to show you, I will coordinate an associate to meet you there.

Our market moves quickly. And so do we.

If you have any questions or need anything at any time, the best way to reach me is via text. Email is also a very effective tool because my assistant monitors that as well. Many times she is able to address the request immediately. Either way, we are here to serve you and make sure that you are communicated with consistently.

Do you work independently or with a team?

I have found what I believe to be the best of both worlds.

First and foremost, when you're doing business with me, you're getting a 25-year veteran agent. As such, I am in-demand, and I can't be everywhere at all times. But I can be right where you need me to be when you need me. I also have a licensed assistant, and she is able to cover for me when necessary and support me and my clients when needed. I am your contact.

How will you determine what homes match my wants and needs?

Perhaps surprisingly…. I won't. I am going to help you determine what's important to you. I will direct you to communities that might be a match. At the end of the day, only YOU can decide what you're looking for.

My strategy is to be the agent to help you get the house you want. For example, I just had clients relocating from California. We started out looking at homes all over the Metroplex based upon their wish list from viewing homes online. Once they arrived here and we were able to focus on what was most important to them, we narrowed their search to four different communities and within those communities, specific houses and floor plans.

We took the 16,000 homes that were available at that time in the Metroplex, and we dialed those down to about 20. And over the course of three days, we were able to view every house that matched their criteria. They were able to pick the right one for them and get it under contract.

Many of my clients are local; they know exactly where they want to be, and they know exactly the type of house they want to have. Once we connect, at their request, I'll go to work creating options for those clients. For example, I may send a mailer to a vetted list of homes in a community that would be a great match for my client. This may very well flush out sellers who are considering a sale but have not yet put their home on the market.

I'm very well-versed on the new construction options in the Metroplex, and have also found that many "for sale by owners" will work with me as a buyer's agent as well.

There are many different sources for finding a house for you. You may very well be the one to *find* your house because you know best what's important to you -- I'll be the one to help you get it.

CHAPTER 8

Your Next Steps

After this tour of all the amenities and the variety of homes and price points, you know that Flower Mound has something to offer everybody. If you're like most people, you're sure to have questions.

I'm Nicole Smith Woodard, and I'm ready to help.

As a lifelong DFW Metroplex resident and in Flower Mound since 2014, and as a real estate professional for the last 25 years, I'm uniquely suited to answering all your queries about this community I've seen grow and change over the years.

I love living in Flower Mound, and I love introducing others to this "big" small town with an ideal quality of life and whole lot more. If something is happening in Flower Mound… I know about it.

I encourage you to contact me at 682-472-2473 or nicole@nicolesmith.net for a free consultation about this community, homes on offer that fit your budget, and more.